Piano · Vocal · Guitar

TOP 25 WORSHIP SONGS

ISBN 978-1-5400-4517-1

Visit Hal Leonard Online at
www.halleonard.com

Contact us:
Hal Leonard
7777 West Bluemound Road
Milwaukee, WI 53213
Email: info@halleonard.com

In Europe, contact:
Hal Leonard Europe Limited
42 Wigmore Street
Marylebone, London, W1U 2RN
Email: info@halleonardeurope.com

In Australia, contact:
Hal Leonard Australia Pty. Ltd.
4 Lentara Court
Cheltenham, Victoria, 3192 Australia
Email: info@halleonard.com.au

CONTENTS

BLESSED BE YOUR NAME

Words and Music by MATT REDMAN
and BETH REDMAN

* Recorded a half step lower.

AMAZING GRACE
(My Chains Are Gone)

Words by JOHN NEWTON
Traditional American Melody
Additional Words and Music by CHRIS TOMLIN
and LOUIE GIGLIO

BUILD MY LIFE

Words and Music by MATT REDMAN,
PAT BARRETT, BRETT YOUNKER,
KARL MARTIN and KIRBY KAPLE

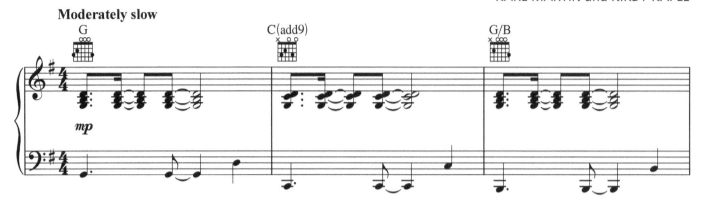

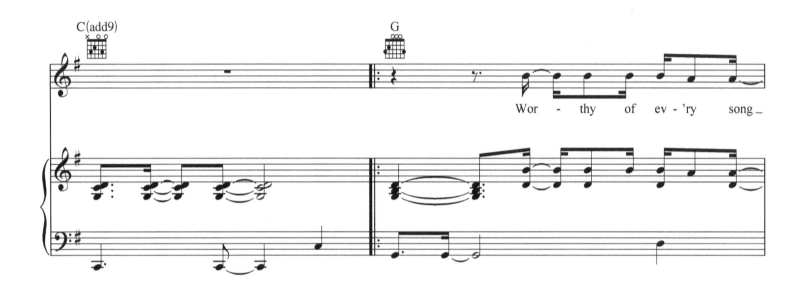

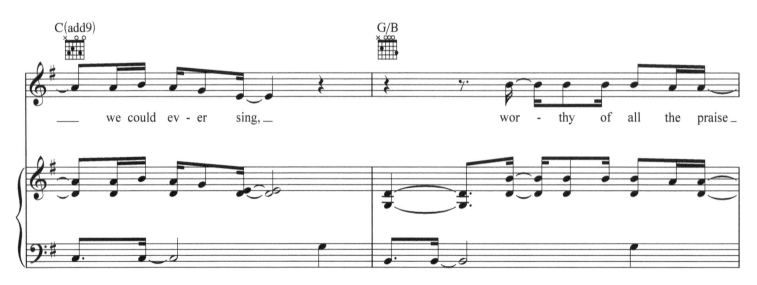

CORNERSTONE

Words and Music by JONAS MYRIN,
REUBEN MORGAN, ERIC LILJERO
and EDWARD MOTE

2
F G C
but whol - ly trust in Je - sus' name.
F Am G C/E
Christ a - lone, Cor - ner - stone; weak made
cresc.
mf
F Am G C F Am
strong in the Sav - ior's love. Through the storm He is
G C
Lord, Lord of all.

GOOD GOOD FATHER

Words and Music by PAT BARRETT
and ANTHONY BROWN

Gently, with motion

GLORIOUS DAY

Words and Music by SEAN CURRAN,
KRISTIAN STANFILL, JASON INGRAM
and JONATHAN SMITH

name, _____ and I ran out of that __ grave, __

out of the dark - ness __ in - to Your glo - ri - ous __ day. __

Now Your

GREAT ARE YOU LORD

Words and Music by JASON INGRAM,
DAVID LEONARD and LESLIE JORDAN

44

HERE I AM TO WORSHIP
(Light of the World)

Words and Music by
TIM HUGHES

48

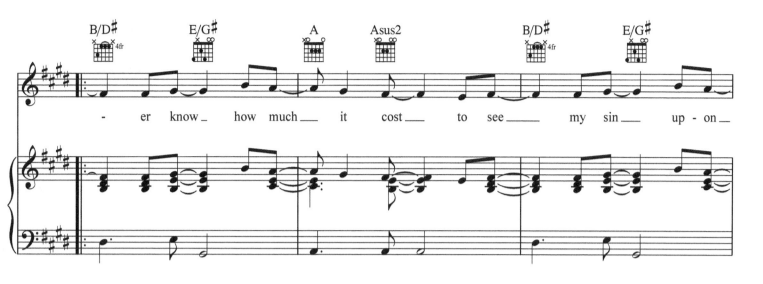

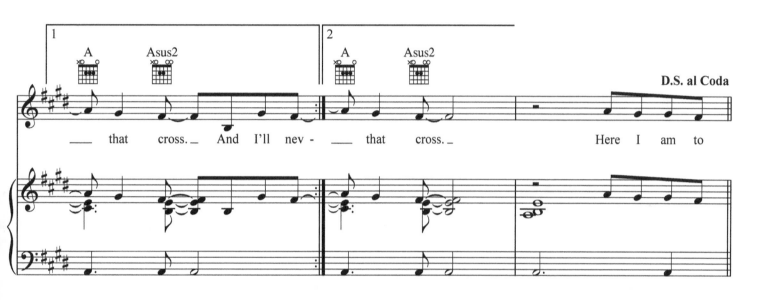

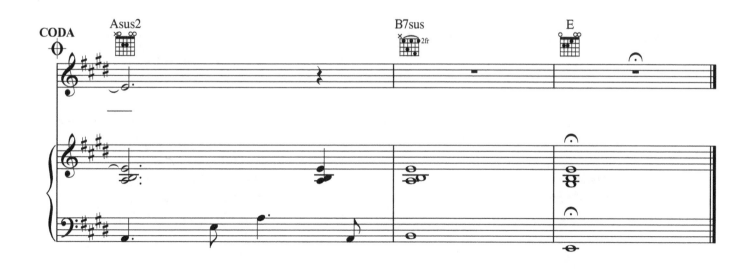

HOLY SPIRIT

Words and Music by KATIE TORWALT
and BRYAN TORWALT

Worship Ballad

There's noth-ing worth more ____ that could ev - er come close.

____ No thing can com - pare; ____ You're our liv - ing hope.

HOW GREAT IS OUR GOD

Words and Music by CHRIS TOMLIN,
JESSE REEVES and ED CASH

With praise

The splen - dor of __ a King, __

age to age __ He stands, __ and

clothed in maj - es - ty. _____ Let all the earth __ re - joice, __

time is in ___ His hands. _____ Be - gin - ning and __ the End,

___ all the earth __ re - joice. __ He wraps __ Him - self __ in light,

___ Be - gin - ning and __ the End. __ The God - head, Three __ in One,

HOW GREAT THOU ART

Words by STUART K. HINE
Swedish Folk Melody Adapted and Arranged by STUART K. HINE

1. O Lord, my God! When I in awe-some won-der _____ con-sid-er
2. woods and for-est glades I wan-der _____ and hear the
3.,4. (See additional verses)

all the *worlds Thy hands have made, _____ I see the stars, I hear the *roll-ing
birds sing sweet-ly in the trees; _____ When I look down from loft-y moun-tain

thun-der, _____ Thy pow'r through-out the u-ni-verse dis-played, _____ } Then sings my
gran-deur _____ and hear the brook and feel the gen-tle breeze; _____ }

*Author's original lyrics are "works" and "mighty."

Additional Verses

3. And when I think that God, His Son not sparing,
   Sent Him to die, I scarce can take it in;
   That on the cross, my burden gladly bearing,
   He bled and died to take away my sin.

4. When Christ shall come with shout of acclamation
   And take me home, what joy shall fill my heart!
   Then I shall bow in humble adoration
   And there proclaim: My God, How great Thou art!

IN CHRIST ALONE

Words and Music by KEITH GETTY
and STUART TOWNEND

63

KING OF MY HEART

Words and Music by JOHN MARK McMILLAN
and SARAH McMILLAN

LORD, I NEED YOU

Words and Music by JESSE REEVES,
KRISTIAN STANFILL, MATT MAHER,
CHRISTY NOCKELS and DANIEL CARSON

THE LION AND THE LAMB

Words and Music by BRENTON BROWN,
BRIAN JOHNSON and LEELAND MOORING

He's com - ing on the clouds;
o - pen up the gates, make

Play cues on repeat

kings and king - doms will bow down. And
way be - fore the King of kings. Our

* Recorded a half step lower.

NO LONGER SLAVES

Words and Music by JONATHAN DAVID HELSER,
BRIAN JOHNSON and JOEL CASE

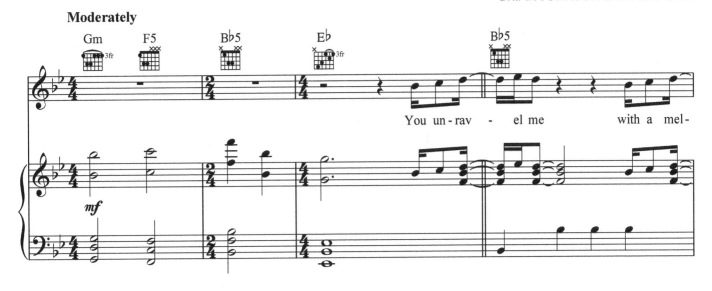

You un- rav - el me with a mel-

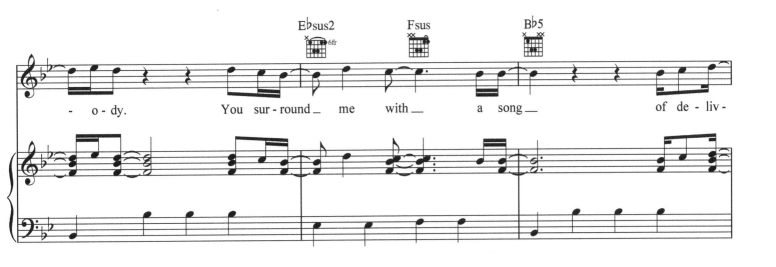

- o- dy. You sur- round me with a song of de- liv-

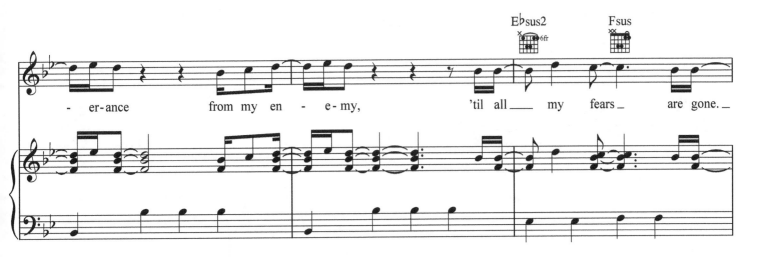

- er- ance from my en - e- my, 'til all my fears are gone.

85

MIGHTY TO SAVE

Words and Music by BEN FIELDING
and REUBEN MORGAN

O PRAISE THE NAME
(Anástasis)

Words and Music by MARTY SAMPSON,
BENJAMIN HASTINGS and DEAN USSHER

Moderately

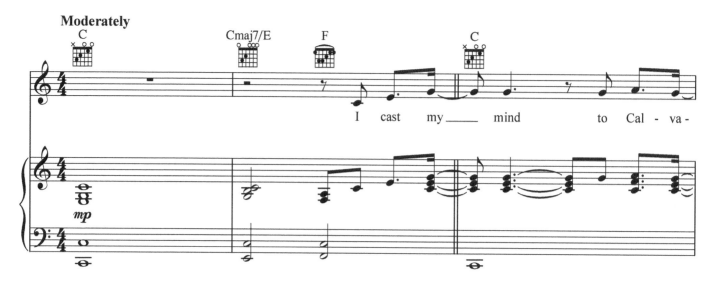

I cast my ___ mind to Cal - va-

-ry, where Je - sus bled ___ and died for ___ me. I see His

wounds, His hands, His ___ feet. My Sav - ior ___ on that curs - ed ___

O COME TO THE ALTAR

Words and Music by CHRIS BROWN,
MACK BROCK, STEVEN FURTICK
and WADE JOYE

* Recorded a half step lower.

OUR GOD

Words and Music by JONAS MYRIN,
CHRIS TOMLIN, MATT REDMAN
and JESSE REEVES

And if our God is for us, then who could ev - er stop us? And if our God is with us,

RECKLESS LOVE

Words and Music by CALEB CULVER,
CORY ASBURY and RAN JACKSON

Be - fore I spoke a word, ___
When I was Your foe, ___

___ You were sing - ing o - ver me.
___ still Your love ___ fought ___ for me.

* Recorded a half step lower.

WHAT A BEAUTIFUL NAME

Words and Music by BEN FIELDING
and BROOKE LIGERTWOOD

REVELATION SONG

Words and Music by
JENNIE LEE RIDDLE

With praise

Wor - thy is the

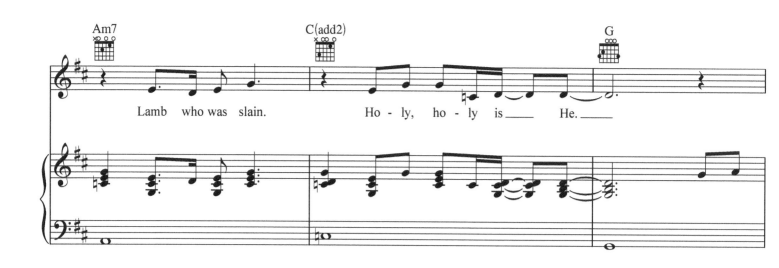

Lamb who was slain. Ho - ly, ho - ly is ___ He. ___

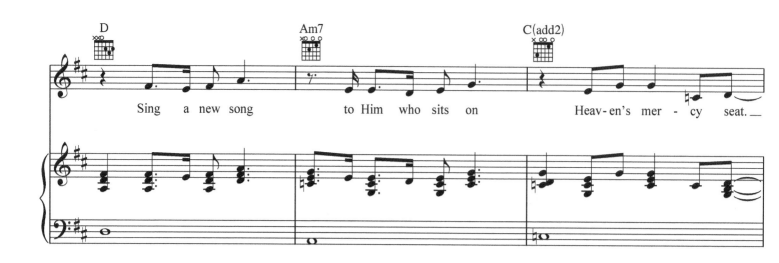

Sing a new song to Him who sits on Heav - en's mer - cy seat. ___

THIS IS AMAZING GRACE

Words and Music by PHIL WICKHAM,
JOSHUA NEIL FARRO and JEREMY RIDDLE

10,000 REASONS
(Bless the Lord)

Words and Music by JONAS MYRIN
and MATT REDMAN